Contents

People have needs

People everywhere have the same **needs**. They need food, clothing, water and homes. They also need to be able to get from place to place.

Where people live makes a difference to what they eat and wear. It makes a difference to their homes and the kinds of **transport** they use.

Why people travel

People travel for many reasons. They
go to work and school. They go to places
to buy or gather things they need.

People also travel for fun. They visit
family and friends who live in other cities
or countries. Some people travel to see
new places or to go on holiday.

Transport around the world

Transport is what moves people or **goods** from place to place. In different places around the world, there are different kinds of transport.

Some kinds of transport can move large numbers of people. Others carry only a few people at a time.

Transporting goods

Many people use **goods** that come from other places. These goods must be moved from where they are made or grown.

How goods are moved depends on what they are. It also depends on their **value** and how far they have to travel.

Transport long ago and today

Transport is always changing. Long ago, people walked or rode on animals. They still do. Today, though, people also travel in faster ways.

Inventions in transport have made travel easier and faster. Riding a bicycle is faster than walking. Travelling by car or another **motor vehicle** is even faster.

Travel using feet

Walking is the oldest way of getting about. Most people travel **on foot** sometimes. Even people who own cars often walk, unless they have far to go.

In some places, people use their feet to move **passengers**. They run pulling little carts, or they pedal bicycles that have small cabs attached.

Travel using animals

In many places, animals are used for **transport**. People ride horses, oxen, camels and even elephants. Sometimes the animals pull carts or wagons with **passengers** inside.

Pack animals are used to move **goods** from place to place. The animals carry parcels, bundles and even large boxes on their backs.

Travel by water

In some places, there are not many roads, or the roads are very crowded. It may be easier for people there to travel on rivers, lakes and **canals**.

Many kinds of boats are used to move people, cars and other **goods**. Some boats go short distances. Others can travel all the way across an ocean.

Travel by road

Some kinds of **transport** need roads.
Many roads are not much more than
dirt or **gravel** paths. Others are wide and
smooth so that it is easy to travel quickly.

Bicycles, cars, buses and trucks travel on roads. In some places there are miles and miles of good roads. People there often travel by **motor vehicle**.

Travel by rail

Trains and **trams** move along on **rails** or tracks. Rail travel is important in large cities. People can travel faster by underground train than they can on crowded streets.

Trains are very important in places where there are few good roads. Some rail **systems** cover short distances. Others go across many different countries.

Travel by air

Planes are used to travel long distances quickly. Some planes carry hundreds of people. Some planes are smaller and carry only a few people.

Sometimes the only way to get somewhere is by plane. In places where there are not many roads, small planes can land in a field. A seaplane can even land on water.

Moving large groups of people

In large cities, many people travel at the same time. Special kinds of **transport** are used, such as buses, and underground and **commuter** trains.

In most cities, many people travel in **motor vehicles**. People do not always use cars and buses, though. Some cities have commuter boats!

In the future

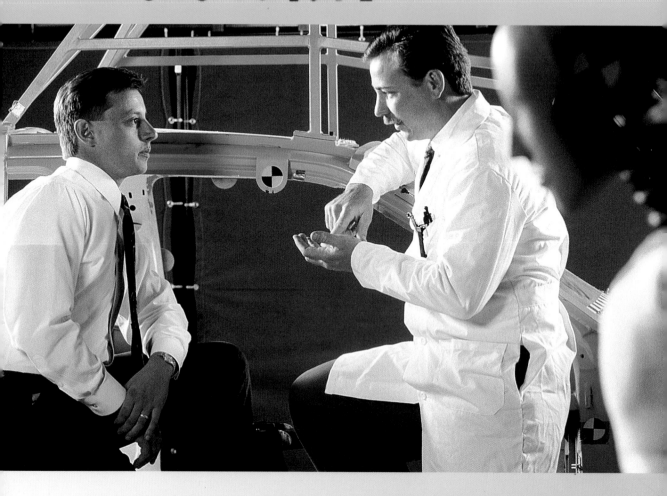

Transport scientists and **inventors** work to find better ways to travel. They think about ways to make transport that is faster, safer and easier to use.

Soon, more people might drive electric cars. Trains might move at even higher speeds. Whatever happens, all over the world people will still be moving from place to place.

Photo list

Glossary

canal   waterway that people have made

commuter   person travelling between home and work

goods   things that will be sold to people

gravel   small stones

invention   useful object that no one has thought of before

inventor   someone who thinks of new ideas and objects

motor vehicle   any form of transport that uses a motor

needs   things people must have in order to live

on foot   by walking

pack animal   animal, such as a donkey or camel, that is used to carry things

passenger   traveller who rides or is carried to where he or she is going

rail   track on which vehicles travel

system   group of things that work together

tram   bus-like vehicle that travels on tracks set into a street

transport   ways to move people and goods from place to place

value   how much something is worth

More books to read

Bicycles by Chris Oxlade, Heinemann Library, 2000

Boats and Ships by Chris Oxlade, Heinemann Library, 2000

Cars by Chris Oxlade, Heinemann Library, 2000

On the Move by Henry Pluckrose, Franklin Watts, 1998

Planes by Chris Oxlade, Heinemann Library, 2000

Take Care on the Road by Carole Wale, Hodder Wayland, 1998

Index